THE STORY OF THE UNITED STATES

THE UNITED STATES TODAY: 1968–PRESENT

by Katherine Krieg

Content Consultant
Eric J. Morgan
Assistant Professor of Democracy and Justice Studies
University of Wisconsin–Green Bay

CORE
LIBRARY

D0010154

Published by ABDO Publishing Company, PO Box 398166, Minneapolis, MN 55439. Copyright © 2014 by Abdo Consulting Group, Inc. International copyrights reserved in all countries. No part of this book may be reproduced in any form without written permission from the publisher. The Core Library™ is a trademark and logo of ABDO Publishing Company.

Printed in the United States of America,
North Mankato, Minnesota
092013
012014

♻ THIS BOOK CONTAINS AT LEAST 10% RECYCLED MATERIALS.

Editor: Lauren Coss
Series Designer: Becky Daum

Library of Congress Control Number: 2013945675

Cataloging-in-Publication Data
Krieg, Katherine.
 The United States today: 1968 - present / Katherine Krieg.
   p. cm. -- (The story of the United States)
Includes bibliographical references and index.
ISBN 978-1-62403-180-9
1. United States--History--Juvenile literature. 2. United States--Social life and customs--To present--Juvenile literature.   I. Title.
372.89--dc23

                                                    2013945675

Photo Credits: Pablo Martinez Monsivais/AP Images, cover, 1; Henry Burroughs/AP Images, 4; Horst Faas/AP Images, 7; AP Images, 10; Bettmann/Corbis, 12; Mittelstaedt/AP Images, 16; Marta Lavandier/AP Images, 18; MTV/Everett Collection, 21; Lauren Rebours/AP Images, 23; Spirit of America/Shutterstock Images, 24; Stephan Savoia/AP Images, 26; Chao Soi Cheong/AP Images, 29; Red Line Editorial, 30, 36; David J. Phillip/AP Images, 33; Ron Edmonds/AP Images, 34; Charles Dharapak/AP Images, 38, 45

Cover: In 2008 Americans elected Barack Obama as the first African-American president of the United States.

CONTENTS

CHAPTER ONE

WAVES OF CHANGE

By the end of the 1960s, the United States looked very different than it had just a few decades earlier. The country saw many changes during the 1960s. Americans took important steps toward equal rights for all citizens. Previously, many rights for African Americans were denied. They had not been allowed to work the same types of jobs or even use the same public restrooms or drinking fountains as

In the 1960s, many people across the country fought for equal rights for African Americans.

white people. The civil rights movement passed laws ensuring equal rights for African Americans.

After the 1960s, the United States faced new changes. It would have to find its place in a world that was rapidly shrinking.

Distrusting the Government

Many Americans were happy that their government was passing laws for equality. But some Americans had other worries about the government.

The Vietnam War had been going on since 1954. That was when Communist North Vietnam invaded non-Communist South Vietnam. In the

The Vietnam War

In 1954 Vietnam was divided into two countries. North Vietnam had a Communist government. The United States stepped in when North Vietnam attacked non-Communist South Vietnam. The United States wanted to prevent South Vietnam from becoming Communist too. If that happened, the United States believed, Communism would spread throughout Asia.

More than 2 million US soldiers traveled across the world to fight in the Vietnam War.

1950s and 1960s, Communism was spreading across the world. The United States worried about the power Communist leaders often had over their people and military. In 1965 the United States began sending troops to Vietnam.

The Vietnam War was the first major war to have television coverage. Many Americans were horrified by the war images they saw on television. Approximately 58,000 US soldiers were killed in the fighting. By the 1970s, many Americans were opposed to the Vietnam War. People across the country held protests against the war. On March 29, 1973, the United States finally removed all troops from Vietnam.

In the early 1970s, another event shook many Americans' faith in their government. On June 17, 1972, burglars were caught breaking into the office of the Democratic National Committee. This was located in the Watergate building in Washington, DC. The burglars were trying to steal information.

At the time, Republican Richard Nixon was president. Nixon claimed to know nothing of the break-in. But in August 1974, Americans discovered Nixon had tried to cover up the burglary. Nixon resigned from the presidency on August 9, 1974.

Struggles and Changes in Leadership

Vice President Gerald Ford became president when Nixon resigned. In the mid-1970s, the US economy was suffering. Prices of goods across the country were increasing. But wages weren't rising to match these higher prices. Ford tried to improve the situation. But more needed to be done. Democrat Jimmy Carter was elected president in 1977, after Ford's term ended. The price of everyday goods was still increasing. Many people were unemployed. Carter had the difficult task of fixing the economy of Americans who distrusted their government's leadership. He helped create 8 million new jobs. This boosted the US economy. But it would take several more years for the country to get back on its feet.

Energy Crisis

In the early 1970s, tension grew between the United States and some countries in the Middle East. Egypt and Syria were Arab nations. The Organization of Arab Petroleum Exporting Countries (OAPEC) refused to sell oil to the United States. OAPEC kept its ban in place until March 1974. This caused huge increases in the cost of gasoline and other energy sources for Americans.

On January 20, 1981, Iran released the remaining US citizens it had held hostage.

Iran Hostage Crisis

Carter also dealt with the country's strained relations with Iran. Back in the 1950s, the United States had supported Iranian leader Mohammad Reza Shah Pahlavi. However, the shah turned out to be a brutal dictator. In July 1979, Iranian revolutionaries broke up the shah's government.

FURTHER EVIDENCE

Chapter One discusses President Nixon and the Watergate scandal. What is the main point of the author's discussion of the Watergate scandal? What key evidence supports this point? Visit the Web site at the link below to read an article about the Watergate scandal. Choose a quote from the article that relates to Chapter One. Does the quote support the author's point about Watergate? Or does it make a new point? Write a few sentences to add to this chapter, using new information from the article.

Watergate Scandal
www.mycorelibrary.com/united-states-today

The Iranian revolutionaries were upset with the US government's support of the shah. On November 4, they attacked the US Embassy in Tehran, Iran. They took 66 hostages. By the summer of 1980, 52 of the hostages were still captive. The remaining hostages were released on January 20, 1981. They had been held hostage for 444 days.

CHAPTER TWO

SUPERPOWER

In 1981 Ronald Reagan became president of the United States. Reagan faced many challenges as president. Many people were still struggling to find jobs. Prices of everyday items were still on the rise.

The Reagan Revolution

Reagan's presidency started an era called the Reagan Revolution. Reagan helped pass laws to fix the problems facing the country. He gave tax

Ronald Reagan was inaugurated into the US presidency on January 20, 1981.

cuts and other support to businesses. This allowed those businesses to create more goods and services. Reagan's laws helped lower prices.

Growing Economy

Other factors also allowed the economy to grow in the late 1970s and early 1980s. Technology was booming. Microsoft created the first personal computer (PC) in 1975. One year later, Apple Computer was founded. Apple introduced its own personal computer called Apple I. Many other companies soon introduced their own models. The digital age had begun.

Macintosh Computer

In January 1984 Apple Computer introduced its first fully assembled personal computer. It was named the Macintosh. Previous computers had been large machines. A team of engineers was usually in charge of running them. The PC allowed individuals to use computer technology in their own homes. When it was first released, the Macintosh cost $2,495. It was one of the first affordable computers.

Becoming a Superpower

Reagan was reelected in 1984. He would face even more challenges in his second term. Since the 1950s, the United States had been at odds with the Soviet Union. The Soviet Union was one of the largest Communist countries in the world. The United States and the Soviet Union were in the midst of a conflict known as the Cold War. This was a period of time in which the countries seemed to be on the brink of war. Both countries had nuclear weapons. Each country was afraid the other would use the weapons to attack.

International Relations

Reagan also focused on keeping the peace between the United States and other nations. Reagan thought the best way to do this was to make the United States very powerful. Reagan increased the money the government was spending on the military by 35 percent. With a strong military, Reagan thought, other countries would be afraid to attack the United States.

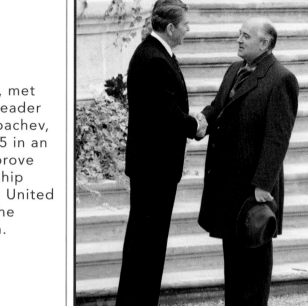

Reagan, *left*, met with Soviet leader Mikhail Gorbachev, *right*, in 1985 in an effort to improve the relationship between the United States and the Soviet Union.

By the 1980s, things had changed. It was clear that Communism was failing in many places. Meanwhile, the United States was emerging as the most powerful nation in the world. By the late 1980s, the threat of the Cold War had diminished.

After World War II (1939–1945) Germany was divided into East and West Germany. Berlin, Germany, was also divided. West Berlin was Democratic. But East Berlin was Communist. A wall was built around West Berlin to keep people from East Berlin from escaping to the West. On June 12, 1987, President Reagan gave a speech to the people of West Berlin:

> *In the West today, we see a free world that has achieved a level of prosperity and well-being unprecedented in all human history. In the Communist world, we see failure, technological backwardness, declining standards of health, even want of the most basic kind—too little food. Even today, the Soviet Union still cannot feed itself. After these four decades, then, there stands before the entire world one great and inescapable conclusion: Freedom leads to prosperity. Freedom replaces the ancient hatreds among the nations with comity and peace. Freedom is the victor.*

Source: Ronald Reagan. *"Tear Down This Wall."* The History Place: Great Speeches Collection. *n.p. n.d. Web. Accessed May 25, 2013.*

Back It Up

President Reagan is using evidence to support his point that Western democracy is better than Communism. Write down two or three pieces of evidence Reagan uses to make his point.

CHAPTER THREE

REACHING OUT

It was the dawn of the 1990s. Some considered the United States to be the most powerful nation in the world. The United States promised a better life to many people in poorer countries.

In the 1990s, the US government passed laws making it easier for immigrants to come to the United States. In the 1990s alone, 13 million people immigrated to the United States. By 2000 there

New US immigrants pledge their loyalty to the United States during a citizenship ceremony in 1997.

Immigrants around the Country

In previous decades, most immigrants settled in California, New York, Texas, Florida, New Jersey, and Illinois. By the late 1990s, immigrant families started settling throughout the country. Many moved away from the popular immigrant states in search of jobs.

would be approximately 31 million immigrants living in the United States. By the end of the 1990s, immigrants made up 11 percent of the total US population.

A New Culture

Immigrants in the 1990s came from countries all around the world. Many immigrants were from Mexico, China, India, Vietnam, and the Philippines. The United States became more diverse. People who had moved to the United States from other countries brought their customs and languages with them. They added to the rich US culture that was developing.

In the 1990s, people were very interested in the media and popular or "pop" culture. Music reached new levels of popularity. Most Americans

Reality television shows, such as MTV's Real World, began gaining popularity in the 1990s.

had televisions in their homes. More sporting events began to be broadcast on television. Cable television became very popular. Many news channels offered 24-hour-a-day news programming.

The Persian Gulf War

The United States had avoided major conflicts with other countries since the end of the Vietnam War. But in August 1990, Iraq's leader, Saddam Hussein, invaded the tiny country of Kuwait. Kuwait shared its northern border with Iraq. Other Middle Eastern countries were worried that Hussein would take their land too. Saudi Arabia and Egypt asked Western countries, including the United States, for help. The United Nations Security Council held a meeting. It warned Hussein to withdraw his troops by January 15, 1991. But the deadline passed. The troops stayed in Kuwait.

On January 16–17, US president George H. W. Bush sent air forces to Kuwait. This air attack was called Operation Desert Storm. The US forces combined with forces from 32 other nations, including Great Britain, Egypt, France, and Saudi Arabia. The forces attacked Iraq by air for six weeks.

The United Nations

The United Nations was founded in 1945 at the end of World War II. It is a group of countries in favor of keeping world peace. The United Nations also works on global issues such as poverty, hunger, disease, and human rights. The United Nations has been a major player in working through many conflicts since it was established.

A US soldier celebrates with Kuwaiti citizens after Iraq's surrender on February 28.

Then, on February 24, ground forces were sent to free Kuwait. In just four days, this mission was accomplished. Iraqi forces surrendered on February 28. The fighting stopped. Iraq promised to follow the United Nations' peace plans. However, issues in the Middle East would continue to have an impact on the future of the United States.

Arkansas's Democratic governor Bill Clinton was elected president in 1992.

The Clinton Administration

In 1992 the United States elected a new president, Bill Clinton. Clinton served two terms as president. During this time, the United States enjoyed a relatively peaceful and productive period. The unemployment rate was low. More people were able to own homes than ever before. Clinton worked to pass laws to improve education, restrict gun sales, and protect the environment.

EXPLORE ONLINE

Part of Chapter Three focuses on the Persian Gulf War. The Web site below includes firsthand accounts of people who were involved in this war. As you know, every source is different. How is the information given on the Web site different from the information in Chapter Three? Is some of the information the same? How do the sources present the same information in different ways? What can you learn from the Web site?

The Persian Gulf War
www.mycorelibrary.com/united-states-today

However, problems between Iraq and the United States continued. Hussein refused to allow UN inspectors to make sure that Iraq was not producing weapons of mass destruction. In December 1998, the United States and Britain launched Operation Desert Fox. On December 16, US and British forces bombed targets in Iraq. The attack lasted three days. US issues with Iraq would continue into the new millennium.

CHAPTER FOUR

A NEW MILLENNIUM

December 31, 1999, was the eve of the twenty-first century. Americans had a lot of questions about what the future would hold. Technology was changing the world. Computers had rapidly entered US households throughout the 1990s. The government had used the Internet since the 1970s. But during the 1990s, it began showing up

Thousands of people turned out in Times Square in New York City to celebrate the New Year for the year 2000.

in US homes. People in the United States could now share goods and ideas more easily with the world.

Many parts of the world were in turmoil. Some US troops had stayed in the Middle East since the Persian Gulf War. The United States was trying to protect its own interests in the Middle East. Some Middle Eastern leaders and citizens were angry about the damage the United States had done during the Persian Gulf War. They wanted US troops to leave.

September 11, 2001

On September 11, 2001, tragedy struck. That morning a commercial airplane crashed into the north tower of the World Trade Center in New York City. Minutes later, another plane flew directly into the south tower. The planes had been hijacked, or taken over, in the air. Firefighters and other rescue workers hurried to save people. Soon both the Trade Center towers collapsed. In the meantime, another plane crashed into the Pentagon. The Pentagon was the military headquarters of the United States.

Americans were stunned and horrified when terrorists attacked the two skyscrapers of the World Trade Center.

A fourth plane was also hijacked. But this plane never reached its intended target. Passengers and flight attendants learned about the other attacks through cell phone calls. They fought back against the hijackers. The plane ended up crashing in a field in Shanksville, Pennsylvania. Everyone on board was killed. Some guessed the plane had been headed for the White House or the US Capitol.

It was later discovered that radical Islamic terrorists were responsible for the hijackings. The attack had been carefully planned. US officials

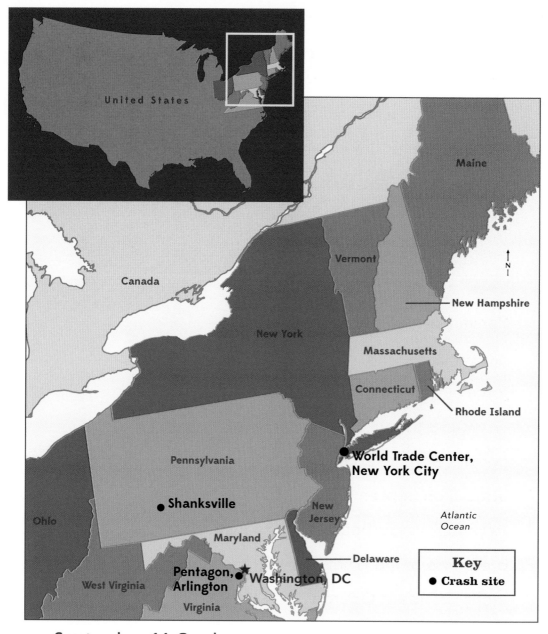

September 11 Crashes

This map shows the cities where four airplanes crashed on September 11. How does looking at the map help you better understand the event? Did you imagine these locations closer together or farther away from one another?

believed it had been planned and paid for by al-Qaeda. This was a terrorist organization led by Osama bin Laden. The terrorists may have attacked because they were upset over the United States' support of their enemy Israel. The terrorists also may have been angry about the Persian Gulf War and the existence of US military forces in the Middle East.

More than 3,000 people were killed in the attacks on September 11. Americans mourned the great loss of life. That night President George W. Bush addressed the nation. He promised to find those who

Operation Enduring Freedom

On October 7, 2001, the US military launched Operation Enduring Freedom. Its mission was to destroy the base of Osama bin Laden's terrorist organization. The military also wanted to get rid of the Taliban in Afghanistan. The Taliban was a radical Islamic group that had taken control of Afghanistan. After two months, the US military had overthrown the Taliban in Afghanistan. But some US troops remained in the country.

were responsible for the attacks. Bush created the Department of Homeland Security to help protect the country from terrorism.

War on Iraq

After September 11, the United States grew concerned about other nations that could threaten the country's safety. The US government believed Iraq had built weapons of mass destruction. Such weapons would have the power to kill many people at one time. On March 20, 2003, troops from the United States and Great Britain invaded Iraq. US troops remained in Iraq until 2011. No weapons of mass destruction were ever found in Iraq.

Hurricane Katrina

In late August 2005, a hurricane hit the Gulf Coast of the United States. It was one of the strongest storms the country had seen in the previous 100 years. Winds faster than 100 miles per hour (160 km/h) hit New Orleans, Louisiana. Many people lost their homes. More than 1,800 people were killed in the storm.

Flooding from Hurricane Katrina in 2005 devastated many Gulf Coast cities, including New Orleans, Louisiana.

Issues in the Middle East were not nearly over for the United States. But the country soon faced more problems at home. The United States economy had been struggling since the early 2000s. Americans would soon meet a new challenge.

CHAPTER FIVE

STRENGTH OF A NATION

In 2007 many people in the United States were struggling to make ends meet. This was the beginning of a large economic recession. The recession impacted the United States and much of the world.

From December 2007 to October 2009, the unemployment rate in the United States increased by approximately 5 percent. The housing market

Barack Obama faced many challenges, including a struggling economy, when he was sworn in as US president on January 20, 2009.

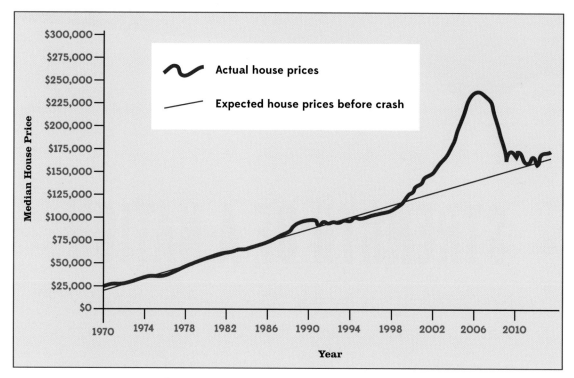

Median House Price

$300,000
$275,000
$250,000
$225,000
$200,000
$175,000
$150,000
$125,000
$100,000
$75,000
$50,000
$25,000
$0

1970 1974 1978 1982 1986 1990 1994 1998 2002 2006 2010

Year

∿ Actual house prices

—— Expected house prices before crash

Housing Market Crash

During the recession, people who had been thinking about selling their homes thought twice. Some people's homes were worth less than they had paid for them. The chart above shows the change in median house values over time. After reading about the housing market crisis, how does the chart help you better understand this issue? What did you learn from the chart that wasn't in this chapter?

also suffered. Banks had loaned money too easily to people who wanted to buy new houses. Many of these people lost their homes when they lost their jobs. As the recession continued, fewer people bought homes. They could not afford them.

A New President

In 2008 Americans elected Barack Obama as their president. He was the nation's first African-American president. He promised to help rebuild the economy.

Obama also wanted to end the Iraq War. It took several years. But the last US troops left Iraq on December 18, 2011. More than 4,500 Americans had lost their lives serving in this war. As the United States left, Iraq worked to rebuild and form a new government. Also in 2011, the United States finally captured and killed bin Laden, who had led the attack on September 11, 2001. News of his death was made public on May 1, 2011.

Obama also worked to create jobs to help with the struggling economy. By the time he was reelected in 2012, there were some small signs that the economy was recovering. But it was clear that it could take several years for the recession to fully end. Obama also introduced health care reforms.

Many people celebrated in June 2013 when the Supreme Court ruled in favor of gay married couples in California receiving the same benefits as straight couples.

These were intended to make health care more affordable for everyone.

Changes and Challenges

The country faced social challenges as well. Gay marriage was one topic dividing the nation. Some people thought that marriages between people in gay couples should be legal. Other people thought marriage should only be between one man and one woman. The decision of whether or not to allow gay couples to marry was determined by each state. By July 2013, 13 states allowed gay marriage.

Environmental issues were also a concern for many Americans. Scientists had noticed an increase in average global temperatures since the early 1900s. But the decade from 2001 to 2010 was the warmest since record keeping began. Scientists realized the earth's climate was quickly changing. It was heating up. This change in global weather patterns was called climate change.

Some people thought human technology was causing climate change. Others thought the change was just a natural occurrence. Scientists in the United States and in

New Energy Sources

In the early 2010s, the United States was working on producing new sources of energy. The country wanted energy sources that were renewable. Renewable energy sources never run out. Wind power and solar power are both examples of renewable energy sources. These energy sources often pollute less than traditional energy sources, such as oil and coal.

Technology Speeds Ahead

By 2013 technology had come a long way from the computers of the 1980s. Computers had gotten smaller and smaller. They were now available in the form of tablets, such as Apple's iPad. Many cell phones had tiny computers. These phones were called smartphones. They allowed people to connect to the Internet from nearly anywhere.

many places around the world began working on this issue. They hoped to discover new ways to create energy that would not cause so much pollution.

Moving Forward

Despite the challenges facing their nation, Americans were hopeful. They continued to look toward the future with a focus on making their nation better.

In 2009 Obama gave a speech at his inauguration addressing the economic recession:

> [We] are in the midst of crisis. . . . Our nation is at war against a far-reaching network of violence and hatred. Our economy is badly weakened, a consequence of greed and irresponsibility on the part of some but also our collective failure to make hard choices and prepare the nation for a new age. . . . Today I say to you that the challenges we face are real, they are serious and they are many. They will not be met easily or in a short span of time. But know this America: They will be met.
>
> Source: "Barack Obama's Inaugural Address." The New York Times. New York Times Company, January 20, 2009. Web. Accessed May 28, 2013.

What's the Big Idea?

Take a close look at Obama's speech. What is Obama trying to say about the state of the country? Find two details he uses to make his point. What do you think is the purpose of Obama's speech?

IMPORTANT DATES

1973

By March 29, all US troops have left Vietnam.

1974

President Richard Nixon resigns because of the Watergate scandal.

1975

Microsoft creates the first personal computer.

1991

On February 28, the Persian Gulf War ends.

2001

On September 11, terrorists connected to the terror organization al-Qaeda attack the United States.

2001

The US military launches Operation Enduring Freedom on October 7.

1977

Jimmy Carter is elected president.

1981

Ronald Reagan becomes president.

1991

On January 16–17, the United States sends air forces to attack Iraq. This is the start of the Persian Gulf War.

2003

On March 20, the Iraq War begins.

2007

An economic recession begins.

2008

Barack Obama is elected as the country's first African-American president.

Dig Deeper

After reading this book, what questions do you still have about the Watergate scandal? Do you want to learn more about the burglary at the Watergate building? Do you want to learn more about President Nixon? Write down some questions that can guide your research. Then, with an adult's help, select some reliable sources that can help you answer these questions. Write a few sentences answering each question.

Surprise Me

This book discusses the many changes in technology since the 1970s. After reading the book, find two or three interesting facts about technology that surprised you. Write a few sentences about each fact. Why were they surprising to you?

Why Do I Care?

The Vietnam War happened more than 50 years ago. But that doesn't mean this history does not impact your life today. How does the Vietnam War affect you today? Do you know anyone who served in the Vietnam War? How might their experience relate to yours?

You Are There

Chapter Three of this book discusses the Persian Gulf War. Imagine you are living in Kuwait when Iraqi troops take over your country. How do you feel when troops from the United States and other countries try to free your country?

GLOSSARY

Communism
a form of government in which everyone shares a country's wealth

economy
the wealth of a country

hostage
a prisoner held by someone who demands something in exchange for that prisoner's release

immigrant
a person who moves to a new country

median
the middle number in a list of numbers from smallest to largest

pollution
substances that are harmful to the environment

radical
in favor of change by extreme measures

reform
to change for the better

revolutionary
a person who works to bring about major changes in something

scandal
a morally or legally wrong event

shah
the leader of Iran

terrorist
a person who uses violence and fear to achieve a goal

LEARN MORE

Books

Crawford, Steve. *The First Gulf War, 1990–1991.* Redding, CT: Brown Bear, 2009.

Pierce, Alan. *September 11, 2001.* Edina, MN: ABDO, 2005.

Wheeler, Jill C. *Barack Obama.* Edina, MN: ABDO, 2009.

Web Links

To learn more about the United States today, visit ABDO Publishing Company online at **www.abdopublishing.com**. Web sites about the United States today are featured on our Book Links page. These links are routinely monitored and updated to provide the most current information available.

Visit **www.mycorelibrary.com** for free additional tools for teachers and students.

INDEX

ABOUT THE AUTHOR

Katherine Krieg is an author and editor of many books for young people. She is currently working toward a master of fine arts in writing.

DISCARD